Behind the White Coat: the things I think and do not say

Volume 1

By Dr. Maiysha Clairborne

ISBN: 978-1-7327525-7-3

DEDICATION

This book is dedicated to:

1. *My colleagues. You are unsung heroes and heroines... You are healers, teachers, mothers, fathers, wives, husbands, sisters, brothers, and caretakers of parents. You are survivors of violence, illness, depression, addiction, sexism, racism, and micro-aggression. You are compassionate, loving, kind, and have crazy work ethic. You are strong for the world, but sometimes not for yourself. You are amazing and you are your worst critic. I could say so much more, but this book is meant to honor you for who you are: people-. living breathing, crying, feeling, bleeding human beings... who just happen to be doctors. I love and appreciate you for who you have inspired me to be for you. Thank you.*

2. *My son. Delsyn, you are the light in my life. You gave me a new life in ways you will never know, and I may never fully be able to express. You are my teacher, my coach, and my best little friend. Your entry into my world was the catalyst for my transition and transformation. Thank you for that. I hope that one day when you grow older you will read this and get a sense of who your mommy is: "the doctor that helps other doctors". Thank*

you for choosing me to be your earthly guide
my little old soul sweet face Delbug.

INTRODUCTION

I remember so clearly how that first experience of burnout almost took my life. And my first experience of what I now know to be burnout was in residency, but back then there was no language for it. I knew something was wrong, b/c I had this thought about 6 months into my intern year, "what did I get myself into...I did not sign up for this". But the reality for me was that I was in too deep to quit (and besides doctors don't quit.... and we'll talk about that later)... and an added layer for me...strong black women don't quit.   So, I kept pushing, and I noticed myself becoming more numb, more disconnected, more sad and sadness turned to depression. But I kept pushing until I found myself one night post call staring down the barrel of a bottle of Percocet that I had from a knee surgery a few months ago, thinking "I can't go on like this" I picked up that bottle. I opened it and stared at those pills, and somehow, I had a moment of clarity. I realized I was not going out like this, and I picked up the phone, called a girlfriend got voicemail and, in a panic, I called another friend. No one was answering, so I dropped to my knees and asked God to please give me the strength to live through the night. That night poetry saved my life. It wasn't the first time (in fact there are at least 3 other critical times I can say that poetry has literally saved my life). I picked up my pen, opened my journal and through tears I wrote... and wrote and wrote...and the next morning I awoke to find that I had survived the night, literally writing myself to sleep. The next day I got help, but that was a defining moment for me: the moment I knew that I could not go on practicing like the factory worker they were training me to be, blindly following orders while completely ignoring what mattered to me. I was lucky. I survived, but my classmate Monty didn't survive. My classmate Sophia didn't survive. And that's why I have dedicated the rest of my career to helping my colleagues create fulfilling careers and fulfilling lives.

This book is meant to be a catalyst for conversation. First, I hope that as you read through it you *feel something.* This is not so much about MY poetry as it is about you connecting to your humanity. I share with you in this book my deepest and innermost thoughts, feelings and experiences. Some of these poems are recent and some of them are older. Through my writing you will get to know me, and my hope is that in some way you will also reconnect to you.

Second, I hope for this book to be a catalyst for conversation out in the community. At the time of publishing this book, I have planned a special event for National Physician's Week to kickstart the conversation, however, my hope is that this conversation will continue and spread; that we will create a community and a movement. The only way to truly shift the way things are currently going is by doing something radical. As you can see this is "Volume 1" and I hope that this is just the beginning. If you enjoy the reading, please share it. At the end of the book will be a guide to how we can continue this conversation out in the community!

Once again, thank you for even picking the book up. That is the first step toward transformation.

Love,

Maiysha

Table of Contents

DEDICATION TO MY SON

Delsyn

His beautiful life
My greatest accomplishment
The Lion of Truth
2017

HONOR THY CHILD

I could have never imagined in a million years

I'd be willingly imprisoned by a love so expansive.

So powerful is the cord that connected you to me

For 10 new moons, that I feel a phantom pain

Where this connection was physically severed

Anytime I walk more than 300 feet away.

You are the light of my life, the love of my universe

And I am but a tiny spec compared to who you are
for me—

My world, my legacy—

And there is this book that says you should honor
me.

But I honor you.

The first 10 months you taught me more than

I have learned in lifetimes, and I had never

Even seen your face, held you in my arms.

Some learn about life watching TV, I learn by

Watching you. 10 months later and you honor me

Simply by existing.

You honor me every time you show me those 3.5
teeth

In the most heavenly smile pull at my heart strings,

You honor me.

Every time you kiss me- open drooly mouth to my cheek

Sweetest reassurance of your recognition of mom,

You honor me.

I can show you the world, but you will teach me how to live

Present in each moment, cherishing the awareness that

When I die I will know that there could be no better life

Because your soul chose me.

So, my beautiful boy, honor me by having a great life.

Travel the world, laugh hard, fall down, get up,

Succeed, Fail, then succeed again. It's all part of life!

Love, grow, Create yesses from No.

Roll around in the grass and laugh some more.

Fall in love with life, Fall in love with love,

And Dance! Play everyday

And in that you will empower others, bring life to the dead.

You will honor me.

Dr. Maiysha Clairborne

Creating life in your aliveness.

Life, like the Swahili translation of me.

In your life, you honor my legacy.

My son, to Honor thy Mother is to honor thyself, and

Create a legacy of your own.

7/28/15

UNCONSCIOUS CONFLICTS

Unconscious conflicts

It is the unconscious conflict
of internal despair that
causes one to provoke another,
the subconscious desire
to be in battle that breeds war.
What do we gain in the fight?
Moreso, what do we lose
without the struggle?
We define ourselves by the
conflict we carry.
The fear of peace is
letting go of the tragedies
with which we identify ourselves.
Losing our identities
by escaping past personal prisons
allows tranquility to create
new paths to
freedom.

© MTC 7/27/05

Dr. Maiysha Clairborne

IMPRISONED MIND

Living in the prison
of my mind, I find myself
contemplating yesterday
When the beauty of
tomorrow is at bay
Dwelling on past
indiscretions and
present ironies
Future indiscreet
possibilities
I've fallen through
the ice too many times
My frozen heart
pollutes my mind.
I stand on a limb
Braced for it to break,
plunging from branches
leaves my
faith at stake.
Multiple infidelities
Trust becomes my foe
I hide behind gregariousness
so no one will know
I embrace cynicism
as my safety net
Thus, the fall
Will be broken with
Each virgin plummet
now I plead with God
Lift away my fear
Letting go of betrayals

with each falling tear
Allowing me to trust
in a much stronger way
Taking baby steps
with each passing day
Surrendering to faith
I relinquish façades
and see my reflection
In the face of God.

© MTC 8/20/2005

Dr. Maiysha Clairborne

BURDEN OF LONELINESS

Today I weep
wishing to die in my sleep
Fantasies of falling away
haunt me
I lay in bed
self-assassination in my head
I pray silently
Deliver me from this iniquity
I reach out my hand
needing someone to understand
To release me from this mental prison
that overpowers me
I pray, I pray
Slipping away
In death,
loneliness is no longer my burden

Let it Begin with me

I am in a warp zone watching
Life go by in slow motion.
It reminds me of a montage.
Buddha is in my ear whispering
for me to be present, and in the
present moment there is so much
tragedy yet I feel a certain serenity,
surreal and almost selfish, but on
the contrary I fully understand my
purpose in this world,
though I don't know what it looks like.
But blindness can bring blessings
and if I just close my eyes and keep
stepping forward I will be led by the
tears of those who call to me.
And if I just open my ears and keep
Stepping forward I will be led by the
Voices of those who will teach me.
And if I just open my heart and keep
stepping forward I will be led by
the grace of a God who loves me.
To know the plan I must walk in faith,
watch crossroads fade into idle existence.
The world keeps passing in alternating
darkness and light; like the scenes of my life
it has always been that way.
Find me, balance; here I am, in lotus
seeking you out, and I cannot hide
from what seems unjust in the world.
But light in the eyes of your child
gives me hope, and light in the soul

of made difference gives me cause.
I continue to put my pieces into the puzzle,
I am a pixel in the bigger picture, picturing
Love and compassion; God give me
vision of your will.
If the collective unconscious can be
Shifted then we will become the
Conscious collective, and
motion through education will
bring balance, let us be the hinge on
which that door swings.
Give me optimism, I am an idealist,
If I cannot save the world,
maybe I can just heal it one
hand at a time.
Hold my fantasy that light years from now
we will be transformed into a higher
Consciousness of compassion,
Less idle ironies and the need to
always take from another's soul.
There will always be enough, unless
we keep using it up.
But if we give, then there will be
Abundance beyond infinite imagination.

I am in a warp zone watching life
pass by in slow motion, and I see its
splendour, fragrant roses bathing in a
background stench, it is all beautiful
So, I will not ignore it.
And when my heart shatters because
I see a 10-year-old dying of leukemia
from bathing in toxic waste courtesy of
the department of sanitation, I will not ignore it.
And when I get a little short of breath because

the shots of a stray bullet pierce the lung
of a barely walking toddler,
I will not ignore it.
And when I bleed for a woman who
has just been beaten unconscious by
her husband because no one was listening
on the other line,
And when an earthquake shakes down an entire
country
devastating an already impoverished people,
I will not ignore it.
I will just continue to reach,
touching one by one and
praying that in my service and
by six degrees of separation,
God will allow my hand somehow
reach theirs too.

12/28/08 (revised 3/16/10)

Dr. Maiysha Clairborne

SEEKER OF LIES

I am the Seeker of Truth
Yet the finder of lies
Deception is poison
In any disguise
I open my heart
And feel only pain
Its venom runs through me
It drives me insane
The price that I've paid
For trusting in man
A knife in my back
Left to die where I stand
A toxic betrayal
Leaves me jaded at best
The smile on my face
Masks holes in my chest
Though my cynical, skeptical
heart remains strong
My soul sees no justice
In righting the wrongs
Holding on to my pain
Takes the peace from my soul
Refusal to relinquish the past
takes its toll
I am the seeker of truth
Laying treasons to rest
Faith and pardon my journey
God, my eternal quest.

THE ELEGANCE OF A BLAMELESS ROSE

Illusion of innocence
a rose hides its thorns,
its fragrant aroma drawing near to it
an unsuspecting victim
Deceptive stunner it punctures
the skin creating a single
drop of blood that falls
from its petals
The reality of its true nature stings
the hearts of all who approach
its false perfection.
Yet captured by its
passionate red wine petals
that are so elegantly
layered over a
heartless center,
they are unable to resist
its sweet pheromones.
And so the coy blossom
continues to prey
Betraying all that call
To its beauty.
The elegance of
the blameless Rose

© MTC 6/29/05

MADD WORLD

ARTIFICIAL HEAVEN

Artificial Heaven
Standing at Hell's door
Awaiting redemption
Craving for more

Artificial Heaven
Faded dreams
Ounces of life fall
From a triple beam

Artificial Heaven
Time stands still
Street light angels cry
Losing their will

Artificial Heaven
Dignity lost
Euphoria gained
But at what cost

Artificial Heaven
Reaching for lies
Selling their souls
For a treacherous prize

No way out
These angels fly
to their Artificial Heaven
A nickel bag at a time

© MTC & SMM 6/18/05

SAN FRANCISCO SLUMS

I walk down the street with
My hands tied behind my back, unable
To do a damn thing about the three men
I just passed sleeping on the sidewalk.
I just gave them the left-over sandwich
That I did not finish from the deli today,
But that will only last them a few hours at most.

The man behind me is talking to himself.
He is a reflection of me
Perhaps it is that which I refuse to acknowledge
That haunts me most.
Is "the man" really keeping us down,
Or is it our own slave mentality?
Probably a little of both...
Sure, I know Capital Hill doesn't share
my passion for healing.
But I continue to heal anyway.

The man behind me is now screaming at his
demons.
Why can't I heal him?
It is the same reason that
Uncle Sam cannot heal this country
It is the same reason that
I cannot heal myself
Fear

The man behind me now weeps
He begs for his freedom
My heart turns to ice, for it is my only defense
against the pain that I feel.

Why can't I heal him?
There is no one to blame.
It is a sickness we all have.
My cell lies adjacent to his; is there a universal key?
Perhaps.

I look at my reflection----
talking to himself----muttering;
I wonder, how did you get here?
Product of society or
product of choice?
There are so many damn products!
I am only responsible for one

6/19/06

THE EYES OF A CHILD

Hey, Can you see what I can see?
How his beating her is affecting me,
Crimson blood dripping from her lip
The bruising on her arms and hip,
Swollen dark circle on her left eye
How my heart skips, when he passes by
Wondering if it would next be I
Wondering if I'm the reason why...
And by daylight no one could see,
His beating her affecting me...

Hey can you see what I can see
How his beating her is affecting me
The alcohol, the drunken stare
Him dragging mommy by her hair
Me stepping on the broken glass
Him threatening "I'll kill your ass!"
And wondering if my baby sister
Could hear or feel when he would hit her
And none of my friends can ever see
How his beating her is affecting me.

Hey, can you see what I can see?
How his beating her is affecting me?
The curdling screams, my splitting hairs
Him pushing us down concrete stairs
The relief of getting away
The horror when we return to stay
The way I hardly sleep at night
Anticipating their next fight
And my teachers can't even see

How his beating her is affecting me.

Hey, Can you see what I can see?
How his beating her is affecting me?
The gunshots as I hold my breath
Did he just shoot my mom to death?
The relief when I hear her voice
The helplessness, the stolen choice
The feeling I can take no more
The 20 Aspirin in the drawer
The grace of God I didn't die
But not because I didn't try
One day she saw what no one could see
How his beating her was affecting me...

Hey can you see what I can see
How his beating her has affected me?
Survivor I can be a voice
Show victims that they have a choice
So grateful that I have my mom
And the strength she passed along
Be inspiration,
Be testimony,
Of how the truth can set you free,
And I can be one who chooses to see
How domestic violence affects
Our community.

09/29/11

OBSERVATIONS ON A TRAIN

A movie, montage of nameless faces---
Isolated stares of strangers on their way to
Their perspective spaces.
I say hi, she says hello, he gives me the Atl nod.
Multiple languages dancing around my ears,
Nostrils picking up various scents of bods;
"Da prisa antes cierra la puerta!"
"Sientate antes te caye!"
"These doors do not rebound or spring back"
Spring back into alternate realities sitting across
from me;
He looks like a serial killer----Ted Bundy.
Better sit down before I fall----fall back into
The arms of some cute guy who you're hesitant
To talk to because you don't know if he's
Parking and riding, or riding and walking.

You know, I think I saw that same woman
On the train the other day-----
She's getting off at West End today.
And me---I ride, turning my head to the window
Watch the fast forward of dogwoods and evergreens
Between industrial parking lots and abandoned
buildings.
"This train is bound for airport station"
I wonder how many people on this train are going
To the airport and why --- mind my own business;
More evergreens, more dogwoods---
More chimneys, more abandoned buildings---
I've been told that as a baby whenever I was
Placed inside a moving vehicle, I'd fall right to sleep.

I'd like to think that thirty-something years later,
I'd grown out of that but (yawwwwn!),
I suppose some things never change.

4/12/10

NOTHING CHANGES

If nothing changes, then nothing changes.
Yes is my default answer and
I will do whatever you please.
I follow the rule of 80/20.
I give 80 percent love
You give 20 percent back.....
Or maybe it's I take 80 percent of your shit
And I receive 20 percent of no benefits.
Whatever the case I'm a masochist because
I always come back for more.
Perhaps it's my steadily descending self-esteem,
Or maybe I'm just a rat on the wheel
Of lost cause.
What exactly am I running after anyway?
Cause it is certainly not love,or respect.
No, I'm running after abuse.
Because it's what's comfortable to me
No, it's just what I'm used to-it's not comfortable at
all.
But if nothing changes, then nothing changes.
If I don't stand up for myself, who will?
If I don't respect myself,
How can I expect the others to?
I can't
I am responsible for taking care of myself
Physically, emotionally and spiritually.
And if I wait for someone else to be my safety net,
I will only fall to the concrete and die.
8/28/2007

THE PLACE

There is a place between
Heaven and hell where souls
Beg for mercy; a limbo where
Spirits learn lessons by sitting
In their own world of in between.
I am sweeping in the hallway of
Nothingness, cluttered with life's
Unmanageabilities.
Black as night, feet stumble over
Old sins, bloody denial covers rage
Suppressed and shelved.
Boxes of self taped up and
Shoved into this hallway, this
Unsuspecting corridor seems
To have no open doors, and no end;
Just clutter-mental clutter in tactile form,
And a broom in the corner.
Time to sweep
Sweep
Sweep away
the dust of denial-.maybe light a candle...
When the choice is made to
Turn on the lights and see the mess,
We can clean it up
One box at a time.

10/8/07

I MEND

Fire like the earth's core. I spit
Icicles from my tongue, piercing
hearts still beating, now bleeding
It started before I was even born.
Blood drips from my lips, the same
Blood that infused my veins,
I am Dracula's love child, sucking
the hemoglobin out of those who dare
to love me , leaving them pale and weakened
but still conscious of the pain.
It was all I knew.
The curse is upon me for generations.
This spiritual death singes my soul,
leaving ashes that form my coated exterior
Obscuring the true beauty that I
behold; instead I hold nothing.
Nothing but fantasy and irrational obsession
My tears create craters in my skin
While the smile remains plastered on my face
I am the Joker, and I jokingly dangle my heart
in the open for all to see but not touch for
it is sterile and I wish it not to be contaminated
by love again.
But life is not a vacuum and somebody sneezes,
sending droplets of love to infect me.
My immune system explodes and the memory of
happiness engulfs me, overpowering neurons
sending electrical impulses like lightning bolts
traveling under my skin I want to shut down now.
But instead I am in overdrive and a warmth
familiar and uncomfortable begins in my

Solar plexus just above my belly button
but just below my breast bone.
I feel expansion and contraction simultaneously,
Now I'm the one who is weak.
My defenses fail me
I see my own blood now coursing through me
Once black, now a deep red again filled
with oxygen, I can breathe again.
And I wonder how the proximity of one being
contains the power to unite fire and ice
Producing the freshest springs
Turn to streams,
Turn to rivers,
Transform into waterfalls
I transform
And I wonder how the love of one person
contains the power to unite fire and ice
Producing the purest springs
Turn to streams
Turn to rivers
Transform to waterfalls
I transform
And I wonder how the grace of one God
contains the power to unite fire and ice
Producing the purest springs
Turn to streams
Turn to rivers
Transform to waterfalls
I transform

3/24/08

ALTERNATE ENDING

He is a child of God,
Strands of hair like Medusa, his eyes wild,
He could turn a lion into stone
He is stoned.
Fighting his demons, the word and the pipe,
He walks the streets yelling epiphanies that could
Only come from God only he can't hear them from
The misting of his mind.
A prophet to others through language,
He resides in a fantasy nightmare that he cannot
Escape, amputating the hands of those who reach
For him, but he calls for more aid.
Tears flow from the eyes of those who meet him
Know him, they love him and he doesn't recognize
The pain of his wounds inflicted.
God weeps for him, waiting for the mist to clear

And for a second, it does. He falls to his knees
In surrender, begging for this monkey's claws
To be removed from his skin, bloodied and wounded
Soul he cries, and a tear drops to the ground
Between his ashen knees, where he finds
A silver dollar that gives him hope...
Hope that this high will be better than the last.
The mist takes over again, and God weeps
Waiting for the mist to clear.

Three days gone, and he knows no difference,
His sunrises and sunsets are a surreal fantasy
Broken reality; between flights he remembers his
son,

And then he remembers the other one...fades back
Into the shadows of the white forest, traveling
sideways
Through rabbit holes, and there is a woman,
A woman who loves him co-dependently,
unconditionally,
His pale princess Bonnie, She lost her virginity to
him again
And together they wreaked havoc, touching clouds,
while robbing people.
They were unstoppable, until the police stopped
Them not too far down the road, now
Bonnie loses her son and Clyde loses his freedom,
But they still have life.
And God weeps, waiting for the mist to clear.

The rusted iron rods slide horizontally revealing
A blinding sunlight that fills his soul with hope.
His steps are heavy with the burden he carries, and
The only outlet he knows is the flow of loud tears
That inspire kindred minds, but can they hear his
cry?
He cries wolf one more time, but he doesn't speak
untruth
This time as the night falls, sharp white teeth, and
the
Piercing claws of that convincing monkey reveal
themselves,
And he is paralyzed. He cannot run. The pain brings
him
To his knees, a familiar posture, and he calls on the
Only thing he knows he has left. He is showered
with
The tears of his Higher Power who weeps for him,
And as the mist threatens to clear, he is faced with
The choice between the inevitable, clarity or death.

27

He has split this thread a thousand times,
Yet, tonight he is like a child again playing
Eenie meenie miney moe with his life.
He picks up the remote control, his hands
Trembling, weakened, and with the innocence
Of a newborn child, he chooses the alternate ending.

5/17/08

GHOSTS

Every time a soul sets sail from a self-inflicted exit
I can smell the odorless fumes of 17 years old, a
musty garage, and that old ford pickup truck.
It's like we're kindreds, those spirits and me
yet I never get to save them from themselves...
Tell them I know the darkness that pulls the morbid
curiosity...no longing for the other side---
tortured thoughts of no one there and
no one to miss me when I'm gone;
pain that you can't exactly put your finger on,
but won't go away...suffocating, and I know it well
Not choking on tears but choking on life
just wanting the pain to go away
just wanting the pain to go away
I thrice was there and once almost succeeded,
the only difference between me and my kindred
departed
is a split second of clarity and
just enough strength to press a button seven times...
Listen for a ring...and a voice
the comfort of even a recorded voice is just enough
to make the difference ...the difference between
a tear stained pillow and a blood stained floor.
Wake up melancholy princess...
the tear stains will dry, but the blood stains will last
forever
in the hearts of those who will never see your
beautiful face again
Hold on a split second longer
Take pause my beloved king, the pain will pass
but the bullets cannot be taken back once passed
through

*the brilliance that is your brain...please hold on just
a split second longer.
Turning clocks back one hour is not enough
to erase the image of your body on the floor----
of tears behind closed doors
Why do we have daylight savings if it doesn't save
time to save lives
Hold on for a split second longer for
on the other side of the dried tears is a light...
the faintest glimmer ----- the softest voice
Let Yahweh whisper strength into your soul as he
once did mine
Give it one more chance... escape death one more
time
Give faith one more chance...and life another try
For many know the comfortable pain of familiar
ghosts
sucking our souls with uninspiring words of
resignation
that it could be no other way, we already have one
foot in the grave.
But I know the peace of mind that comes with
"anything is possible"
And where we may all be one breath away from
extinction
We are one conversation from freedom
5/27/13*

LIKE GNATS

Gnats---dancing frantically in the sunlight, and
It reminds me of people--- chaotic and frenzied,
Randomly and mindlessly creating beautiful
Formations of possibility, but then scattering
At the hint of opportunity for something bold
And beautiful to occur.
They stare---just long enough for the butterfly
To pass them by and reach its perceived horizon;
Then it's back to frantic living.
Who has time for beauty anyway, when
There are so many obstacles in the day.
When there are households and corporations
To be run; when status updates and tweeting
Must be done; when you're caught up
Instant messaging someone. Who has time for life?
I mean, who even has time for a husband or a wife?
That circular band around your 4th finger left hand
Is only there to remind you that somewhere in a land
Far far away (called your home), there is only your
Perfect complement waiting, along with mini-versions
Of your combined DNA, also updating their statuses,
Tweeting and messaging by the way.
You just read that your kid conquered the 4th world
in
Final fantasy when he's supposed to be
Conquering trigonometry---so you comment on his
Facebook page

Do You know why the sky is blue?
It's because blue is supposedly the shortest
wavelength

31

And when it scatters and reflects it just happens to be
The one wavelength our eyes can see.
It's called Rayleigh's scattering; and
It reminds me of how we scatter.
Attempting to take the shortest distance
To our destination instead of enjoying the journey on the way.
It seems the destination is all we care to see...
And if we are working toward the shortest distance to death
We may be well on our way, however
If happiness is the final destination we seek,
We may want to re-think our strategic short cuts...
Like Gnats;
We may want to dance frantically in the sunlight
Creating beautiful formations, but with awareness.
Put down touch screens and actually touch things—and people.
We may want to get back to date nights, and watching
Pay-per-view fights with chips and dip and
Vulgar tongue slips while talking a little smack to the opposing team.
We may want to enjoy potlucks with friends and delicious
Meal blends followed by cuddling up in front of the TV
And watching a great movie.
We may want to relish playing together, and
Treasure praying together while sitting around the Table for a family meal.
Be still
But live life.
And dance frantically in the sunlight.
Because the day after tomorrow could be

*The day that Your Earth
Stands Still.*

9/6/10

ODE TO FLOWER PAINTING

There you shine through a
Reflective glass house displaying
All of your brightness and beauty.
Originating from the earth
You inspired some granola guy
With a tam to dig feverishly into
Their heart and soul and then into
Their oil bases repeatedly replicating
Your vibrance and charm.
Oh, flower upon the wall!
You sit boldly between your siblings
Commanding attention with curves
That move my eyes like the pieces on a boardgame,
Slowly and methodically, strategizing
Stopping over every detail.
Yours are the primary colors,
Proving you are in the forefront
Commanding respect and letting
All whose eyes shall fall upon you
That you will not be ignored.

2/13/10

COLLECTIVE CONSCIOUSNESS OF CRAZINESS

We have this collective consciousness of craziness,
When crazy ex-girlfriends point pistols for
Forgetting birthdays ----
But why was he hitching a ride with her
To pick up his son anyway.
Mixed signals become very clear
When facing a bullet filled barrel, I'm sure.

Collective consciousness of craziness,
When neighbors noticing new flat screens
From burglarized houses allow officers
To claim them and turn them into "police property".
She probably never would have been suspected
If she had just discretely moved the TV
Into her living room....now, instead
The entire police station enjoys a crystal
Clear view of ESPN and Sunday college football.

Collective consciousness of craziness,
When road rage turns scalding because
Someone hurls hot coffee in morning traffic.
"She just wanted to change lanes!"
Well, maybe throwing something at
some else's car to let them know that you
want to cut in front of them is probably
not considered effective communication.

Collective consciousness of craziness
When blind burglars break jaguar windows

To steal only what they truly need;
A $100 pair of prescription glasses.
I guess he REALLY wanted to be able to read
The Sunday Paper....
And they say we don't need healthcare reform

The world is an intelligent place, but
When human stupidity gets mixed with
Emotion and perceived scarcity,
(And Possibly when the moon is full, and
Mercury is in retrograde)
Beware! Because,
The collective consciousness of craziness will
Be just around the corner waiting to rear
Its dubious unhinged head!

1/9/10

ON LOVE, LUST, & RELATIONSHIPS

SUCCULENT MAN

Peanut Butter & honey
was my favorite combination
until you came along.
The nectar of our union
created a far more interesting taste.
An unlikely fit, I must admit;
Your tortuous path traveled
almost divinely to meet mine.
And by the way, I knew that day
that you were watching me as
I walked away---
That's why I walked ...so....slowly.
It wasn't the day we met but
eight weeks gone that I was eating
my own bitter words;
"I will never date a man who....."
These words did not go down
with ease, in fact eight full months passed
 prior to full digestion; and
I regurgitated them from my subconscious
with every new exotic flavor you released
(And there were plenty).
But even so I was sure after only eight weeks
of knowing you that there could be,
NO, there WOULD BE
NO ONE ELSE with whom
I would share a six month relocation

across the globe.
Now isn't that interesting?
So, fighting the inevitable acceptance

of my affection for you, I added you
to my mixing bowl (in sprinkles of course);
I let you in, and together we
explored the world in each other---
Like children---experiencing a growth
so profound that even the Dali Lama
himself might be proud.
It was the best feed of my life
We were---we are
a savory fusion of succulent truth
the sweetest combination I have
had yet to enjoy.
And though the imprint of my
original gustatory sense remains
in clear existence,
I would rather not imagine
what life tastes like without you.

MTC 6/1/06

HERE WE GO AGAIN

"What's this?
I found it in your pants
Oh! Cut the song and dance
I've called her in advanced
I sigh
"Don't lie
I know your little game
Don't try to act ashamed
Just tell me what's her name?"
I'm struck
He's stuck
"She told me it was Zoe,
of me she didn't know.
It's time for you to go.
I turn
He grabs
"Don't 'wait' don't 'babe' me
You had your chance, you see
Not one, not two, but three!"
I sob
I yell
"My love for you was deep
But now I feel so cheap.
What you sow you will reap"
I'm pissed
I ache
It feels so damn injust
How can I learn to trust
When what drives him is lust
I'm done
I'm through

"The fault I will not take
You knew what was at stake
And you chose to forsake"
Deep breath
I walk
"You cannot rectify
I will not crucify
I'll simply say goodbye"
The door
Slams shut.

© MTC 01/23/2006

Dr. Maiysha Clairborne

LIES

The lies flow
So effortlessly that you wonder
'Does he believe that?'
'Should I?'
The untruths cascade,
Each locution more false
Than the previous one.
Continuously misrepresenting,
Perjuries leak from his lips.
Quite convincing are his
Confabulations and creations.
Not unlike the tales of Aesop.
But the storyteller becomes
The snare of his own fictitious life,
And his inveracities, inevitably
Leave him standing alone
In the crosswinds
Of Karma.

© MTC 01/23/2006

HE STANDS BEFORE ME

He stands there waiting,
Waiting to catch me as I fall.
Like the Kauri tree his soul is a
thousand years old and he stands firm
His eyes piercing, piercing me with
His unconditional love as he watches
Me transform
I transform
from rage to nothingness and my
normally silent cry becomes like a
wolf on a full moon, or like
a mother who has lost her only child,
wailing, streams turn to rivers and the pain
builds so much so that I feel my heart
expanding in my chest as if it is going to explode
and then contracting violently sucking my
whole world into its emptiness.
His hand rests on my back, a warm touch
A surge of compassion I shrink like
a weeping willow.
And just before my heart turns to ice,
just before I lose faith in who I am he whispers,
"I love you"
Bringing sobs to a soft whisper
I look into his eyes, piercing
Piercing me with his unconditional love.
He doesn't judge me
He just stands there waiting,
Waiting to catch me as I fall

43

Firm like the Kauri tree his soul a thousand years old.
He has always been there waiting to catch me
But today, I finally let him.

MTC 1/2/07

SPEAK

I want to make love to an unaltered mind
Free of worry and shame and
Clean of blame.
How your kisses taste like lies...
How my caresses are filled with condemnation.
Can I simply touch you gentle and
Can your whispers be absent of secrets and street
pharmaceuticals.
We co-exist independently in our own permissions.
I forsake you first before you abandon me
For some quick hit that you get down the street
From the Quicktrip.
We sit poised and stifled, watching the Variations
Of positions that we wish to encompass in this
awkward moment.
Our wall of truth is splashed with abashment
And I am taken aback by how uncomfortable we are
As we try to force this solution,
Sex is obviously not the answer.
Neither of us really knows what to say,
And I want to get up and run away,
And you want to try to make me stay
And we become this silent tornado,
Swirling, confusion, chaotic communication
Of nothingness bouncing blindly over
Critical perplexities and unspoken uncertainties until
The core of what we originally united for is spoiled
Leaving us emotionally bankrupt and
Spiritually shattered.
We each lie in our own puddle of shame and low self
esteem.

But we want to make love despite our abasement,
We want to make love anyway.
We want to dissolve that wall, turning contempt into
connection.
Transforming tears of unease into uninhibited,
unaltered ecstasy.
We have the power and all we have to do is look at
each other.
Look at each other without contempt, fear and
abomination.
All we have to do is look at each other,
Look at each other without judgement, shame or
entitlement.
All we have to do is look at each other
Look at each other
And Speak.

06/2007

MISSED OPPORTUNITIES

Missed opportunities rush by me
Like a cold blizzard breeze causing
A chill to my bones, my heart chakra
Swells, and I close my eyes to catch
My balance. They stand there perfectly still
As if just placed on top of their own
Wedding cake for everyone to see.
Her love for him envelops the room.
It pierces me. I let it run through.
She is reflected in his contentment.
He is happy, he is relieved;
He looks at me and smiles.
My solar plexus warms, and
I intuitively nod and mouth to him
"You are beautiful"
he mouths back, " are you okay?"
with my hands in prayer at my
breaking heart, I bite my lip and
smile through tears, "No!" I want
to scream, "I love you!"
But instead I lovingly nod my head
And whisper back to him "Yes".
It's true, I love him;
I am in love with him.
But his happiness is most important to me.
And missed opportunities puncture my
Skin like a million small needles.
I can no longer bear the pain, so
I allow the dam to crack.
Mixed emotions flood me,
The love I have for a man that I can never tell,

The loss of a man I can never have,
The joy I feel for a man I can never stop loving.
It is a pattern that has often been repeated
In my life for as long as I can remember.
I move through times like H.G. Wells
Remembering the bliss that was once
My own wedding, then the fear that
Ensued when I realized the fallacy of
Our union.   In actuality, I grieved
The end of our matrimony before I
Walked the aisle. Factuality
Revealed itself 3 months later, the
Cracks in the foundation finally
Taking down our own castle.
Now I stand in someone else's memory.
Back at the reception, I watch them.
He gently brushes a stray hair from her face,
His adoration of her evident.
The rumba in their first dance reminds me
Of the tango in mine.
Memories rush back of how beautiful
My day was, and how it so soon came to
A heartbreaking halt.
And now his hand overlaps hers
Cutting a piece of their rich red velvet
Future with all to share.
Just as 6 months ago I cut mine.
We sliced our chocolate butter marbled
Hereafter and fed sweet superficial
Beauty to each other and 60 witnesses.
We danced with each other like they danced,
A stunning performance that even we could
Only keep up for so long.
And now at the wedding of another
Missed opportunity, I dance with the
Golden groom, not my own.

I feel his soft skin on mine and I
Know it will be the last time.
He asks me if I approve of his new love.
And though I want to tell him that she
Is only the next best thing to me, I simply
Say yes.
We lock eyes and for a few seconds
I step out of my body and into his.
I hear him silently tell me he loves me too.
With only the beat of his heart, and his
Breath on my cheek.
And as we break our gaze, and then our hold,
I let him go, and I am happy for him.
He has found his complement.
And now missed opportunities become
Open doors to infinite possibilities.
I move gratefully to my future with a
Steady confidence. I show up and
God meets me there. I know that there
Is no fear in being alone, only strength.
And abandonment is only an illusion
Fed to me by people that didn't know differently.
I know that the most important force to trust
Is God and the most important person to trust
Is myself. That the more I grow, the less I know
And that I can lean on my Almighty Yahweh
For the rest. That I already have all the love
In my live that I will ever need, because I love
myself;
Finally, I know that missed opportunities
Mean nothing because God's timing
Is always the right timing and when I am
Spiritually, emotionally, and yes financially
Whole, that missed opportunity will
Return to me as an unimaginable future.
10/29/07

THAT MOMENT

My plane touches to the ground at 3:00
And yours takes off at 4:00
My heart all but explodes as they
Open up the door.
I almost leave my bag
But it has your favorite book.
I stop by the ladies room
To freshen up my look.
I check the screen Flight 515
I'm on to concourse D.
Forget the train it's way too slow
It's quarter after 3:00
My heart beats faster than my feet
Imagine that they could go.
I'm walking fast as I can walk
But still it's just too slow.
I finally reach the concourse,
Now I'm running to the gate.
It's been too long since your embrace,
I hope I'm not too late.
I run to you we share a kiss
And then you take my hand;
Down on one knee you ask to be
Eternally my man.
The voice announces overhead
Before I can reply.
The words are trapped within my throat,
All I can do is cry.
The answer and our time is up
You rise to board the plane.
My broken heart, my finger gleams,

I watch you leave again.

7/14/08

THE DANCE

He's pulling me close.
He wants me to stay.
His grip slowly tightens.
I'm slipping away.
Distress inundates me,
I can't comprehend
the pain of his tone
He doesn't intend.
The pain of his words
which he's unaware,
mutes out my desire and
blankens my stare.
He tightens the noose
devotion in mind,
He tells me he loves me
I respond in kind.
He tells me he loves me
I know this is true,
I sit on my cold feet
'Cause I love him too.
But misread intentions
and old healing wounds
imperils our bond
endangers foredoom.
What strength do we have now
If we don't have God,
and if we keep hiding
behind our façades?
No trust in the process
leaves no confidence
to trust in each other

without recompense.
Our path now obscured,
persist we our quest
to fight for this rare jewel
in which we invest.
Accepting enigmas
will dissolve our gloves.
We want the same ending
to consummate love.
12/30/07

GOOD TIMES

Love me like you do
Like others wouldn't think to.
Play in my hair,
Rub my feet,
Hold me while I cry
when I'm mad at you.
It's the little things you do
Like locs lifted from my face
while chunks of undigested last meal
miss the porcelin god,
but not your feet.
Bring me soup.
Carry me to bed.
Kiss me on my forehead.

Walk me to work.
Start dinner before I get home;
Learn how to cook...no prepare.
Draw my bath;
Wash my back.
Watch my back.
Watch chick flicks.
Watch flicks of chick on chick.
Bring toys to bed.
Push me to ecstasy.
Pull me on stage.
Stage scenes of laughter.
Profess love unabashedly
publicly and privately.

Say yes to the unknown.

Fly across the world on a whim.
Jump off a crane connected
Dance with the Maori.
Eat with strangers.
Chase sheep.
Pet llamas.
Eat ostrich.
Watch the same 3 shows
every day for 1/2 a year.

Photograph full moons.
Swim with dolphins.
Kayak angry oceans.
Climb to god-like mountain tops;
Get lost in horizons.
Watch golden suns rise.
Walk beaches at sunset.

Stroll the mall
People watch
Make up their lives
Make up our lives
Pretend to be dramatic
Fake fuss and fight about nothing
Be ghetto fabulous
..."And scene!"

Laugh until we cry
Cry until we laugh
Talk until we resolve it
even when "we" are no longer we
but just you sitting across from me.
Whole and Complete.
Gratefully remembering.
The mutual contribution,

layers of unexpressed authenticity unleashed,
Knowing how the experience
of the love we had gives
new context for creating an
Unimaginable new future.
Yeah….Good Times.

8/17/15

SILENT CONVERSATIONS

A. M. A.

This year is a very special year.
In This glorious year of 2010,
I will officially be A.M.A
Advanced Maternal Age.
At first mention this sounds
somewhat dismal, I mean
the medical definition of A.M.A is
the age at which carrying a pregnancy becomes
"high risk" – 35
where the potential for birthing
a child with Down's syndrome goes up
by approximately 10 – 20 %
(depending on what age you're starting from)
and each passing moment after the ovaries just get
older...and older....and older!
A very special year indeed, this
Advanced Maternal Age.

But four and a half decades of life
Surely doesn't simply translate to "old mom"
No, not to me.
I mean, let's break the real meaning of this A.M.A
Starting with....
Define Advanced –
The state of being of a higher level in knowledge
And skill; ahead in development
Complex and intricate... Enlightened
So really you could say
I'm becoming a new and modern,
Up to date, progressive,
pioneering and innovative

Sophisticated mom....avant guard!
Define Maternal –
The quality of having or showing tenderness,
Warmth, and affection
(I've got that)
The lioness is devoted to her cubs
Nurturing and protecting them to death,
Or at least until they're grown
Advanced and Maternal

Like Mother Theresa,
Who may not have had any
Biological offspring, but sprang
Her love and grace to thousands
Of children in need of nurturing.
A simple sophisticated passion
Of compassion and we overlook that.
Like Pema Chodron, whose
Seemingly progressive spiritual orations
Are actually ancient spanning generations,
No dynasties...embodiment of Buddha,
Spiritual advancement in the simplest
Concept that the end of suffering
Is possible through detachment
And unconditional love.

Like Isis, Goddess of Simplicity
Representing motherhood, magic,
And fertility. "She" literally "of the throne"
Answering petitions of lost children,
Protecting memories of fallen mortals
Conceived from the unions of the earth
And the overarching sky, her tears
Flood the Nile and the lifeless ask why,
For she is the ideal mother and wife,
Patron of nature and giver of life,

Advanced and Maternal
And I would say that Earth is the
Original mother, so if this is the
Epitome of A.M.A, I'll take it.
For she breathes life into all whom
Even lay eyes on her;
Bounty infinite, nutritive spirit
Without the Maternal Earth, we would
All be withered away in sickness and death.
Even at a billion years of age,
She still looks beautiful.
And even through the abuse and neglect
Her children give her.
She Continues to birth unspeakable works of art;
She adapts, she endures, she evolves;
Advanced and Maternal....

Hmmmm. Doesn't sound so horrible anymore;
A.M. A now feels more like
Alluring Maternal Asset or
Accomplished Matriarchal Alchemist ---
---Transforming "old moms" everywhere ---
Our over 35 nature is just fine,
We get better with age just like good wine---
Okay, Okay, to cliché!
How about like wisdom, life stories, and body image;
Like vocabulary, self awareness, and common
sense;
Like sex, patience, and self esteem;
Life real estate, mutual funds, and living dreams.
It all just gets better with age!
So, bring on this A. M. A
2010 is going to be a
phenomenal transformation after all.
Now if I could just get a husband!
12/31/09

WORTHY

I am not worthy
Why? Because I was an honor student in high
school.
Because,I struggled through college determined to
take my education
to the next level and because I succeeded.
Because I graduated with high honors from medical
school. Yet I cried myself to sleep every night
wondering why I felt such isolation,
when I had no cause, no right to feel this way.

I kept telling myself
I am not worthy

At age 12 I watched my mother being dragged up
the grass by her hair.
At age 13 I watched her pregnant with my baby
sister being doused with lighter fluid, followed by
her head being shoved into our fireplace.
At age 14 shots rang out in the middle of the night
and I held
My breath waiting to hear hers. Had he finished her
off this time?
A weekly cycle of chaos, for 10 years I endured. Was
I to blame?

And I kept telling myself
I am not worthy

Violence was the only outlet I knew, so
I attempted my first suicide at age 12, my second at
age 17.
I drifted away inhaling carbon monoxide deep into
my
Soul, my altered mind finding peace in this
permanent escape.
It was an escape that I would desire over and over
again, for life
Was just too painful and death was a much better
option.

And I kept telling myself
I am not worthy

I am comfortable being unworthy. It allows me to be
in a state
Of darkness. I fear enlightenment because with it
comes responsibility
I fear success because with it comes expectation
And how can I hold the expectation that I am
beautiful.

So I keep telling myself
I am not worthy

Being unworthy is part of my identity and being
depressed
is all that I know. I am privy to being in self pity and
I am terminally unique. My self loathing is crucial to
my existence and
It is my own fear that suffers me to maintain
This most distorted process of thinking

Then a voice whispers to me
You are worthy

*But If I confess to my worthiness then I will have to
step
Out of darkness and into illumination, I will have to
step
Out of selfishness and into vulnerability. I will lose
my identity
 but I will gain my freedom. I will realize that I am
the only one
holding myself back from true enlightenment.*

*A voice whispers to me
You are worthy*

*But, If I admit that I am worthy, then I will have to
love myself
And value myself, look in the mirror and see
perfection that is the image and likeness of God. I
will have to become
The Divine being that I am. And recognize that I am
She
And She is me. Yahweh open your arms and
swallow me whole.
 What am I waiting for?*

*A voice whispers to me
You are worthy
I am awakened and made conscious. Made whole
and made anew
And I am made aware that the voice that speaks to
me is my own.*

MTC 08/27/06

SEARCHING

I am a detective searching for my soul.
Trying desperately to solve this case as
I study in the mirror this stranger's face.
Who are you?
I thought I always knew.
But the forensic evidence was inconclusive
And I, the culprit, was so elusive that the
Investigation had to continue.
I am a detective searching for my freedom.
Although I thought all along I had been free
I realized I was hiding inside of me.
Oh how tricky, tricky this whole spiritual
Growth process can be
The more I learn, the less I see.
I am a detective searching for a solution.
I am searching for a spiritual evolution
And for a personal revolution.
But I must first escape my own
Personal persecution.
Because the only one who stands in my way is me
And it's really God's face in the mirror I see.
So instead of always desperately trying to flee
Well....case closed

3/10/07
.

PROGRESS, NOT PERFECTION

She was told 'Progress, not perfection'
But it didn't feel like progress to her
When she heard her ceramic elephant
Smash against the bedroom wall.
The moment it left her grasp, she gasped.
"what is this feeling?" she asked
It was familiar but unfamiliar as
it only appeared in surges.
She never knew how to feel anger.
It was classified as an emotion she
was not allowed to experience.
So it only appeared in surges.
Like the surge of blood that poured
from her wrist as she cut,
Like the surge of carbon monoxide
as she inhaled toxic fumes into her lungs
She was not allowed to feel.
So when the ceramic elephant
left her grasp she remembered.
She remembered all the times her
chest welled up only to collapse.
She remembered why she never screamed
Only whispered
She remembered why she never cried,
Only wept.
And it all came crashing down
Like the little pieces of that oversized figurine
That had been gifted to her
Anger had not been gifted to her.
So she used the elephant as a surrogate
For all the pain she wanted to feel but
never could and she let it go;

She let that elephant go.
And the feelings rushed in,
And the feelings rushed in,
And the feelings rushed in,
Until her heart began to explode
Until her soul began to implode
And from her came a roar so thick
That even she crumbled to the ground.
She let that elephant go.
And suddenly she could breathe
And suddenly she could could cry
And suddenly she could see.
And she became this beacon of self honesty.
It consumed her and from her face
Rivers of relief created oceans from wells.
She let that elephant go.
They told her progress not perfection.
And even though anger didn't seem
like progress to her, she knew
it had to be a start
to feel anything close.

3/18/07

FREE WRITE #112

When the moon creeps over to blot out the sun,
A shadow falls over the spirits of many.
Emotions wrestle with the planets
Tugging fiercely back and forth, feet in
quicksand leaving imprints like idiopathic reasons.
A tear falls on an upside down couch, and a scream
belts through muted speakers. Chaos toxic
like radiation disseminates through pipes
in the water contaminating all who drink or shower.
Feelings metastasize, planting little seeds of
Fear into the most remote areas of my mind.
She makes you think you're crazy when it never
used to be this way. Shattered intuition trickles
into robbed self-esteem and he wonders why
She can't stand to look at him.
He is the mirror. No taking responsibility
Only blaming circumstance because it's too
Hard to blame each other.
No commitment to quit for it would be too
Hard to face reality. So they keep swirling
The drain but never going down. The insanity is
almost ten-fold.
They are masochistic for each other.
Dive off the building and feel the free fall.
Then and only then will you know the comfort of
A safety net.

8/29/07

OPEN WOUNDS

Take a look at these wounds, they run deep;
Cutting through flesh, tendon through bone
Reaching the core of my empty body and
Coming out of the other side, and for the
Last seven months I've laid down my pride.

Take a look at these slits on my wrist.
They are not self-inflicted but created
By lies, knives thrown at me by masked
Murderers of the soul, pretending to be my friend
And my husband.

Take a look at these dripping lines of blood.
A horizontal intersecting a vertical
Forming a cross not representing Christ
But signifying crossroads.
I have been here many times before,
The other woman knocking at my back door.

Take a look at my face, lines heavy forming
Like lines on my wrist forming layers of
Scars that don't come out with laser or
Microdermabrasion. They connect to
Neuronal pathways lighting up every time
I've ever had a man or woman chop away
Another piece of my sanity, my trust, my dignity.

Take a look at my bloody hands clasped,
Pleading with my God to please lead me
On the right road this time. My knees are ashy
And callus from dropping down on them more

Times a day than a blessed Muslim.
I pour every ounce of myself onto God's
Sacred ground in faith that this too
(my pain) shall pass, but
hoping maybe instead God will just
put me out of my misery.

Take a look at my life, perceived to have
Achieved yet dunked into a chaotic and
Dishonest silence. Hung by the neck in
The crossfire of addiction yet a willing
Participant in my own demise.
I didn't cause it, I can't control it,
And I can't cure it.
But I have choices.

And I stand here with my choices
Struggling to breathe in my own pool
Of blood at this very familiar place
Without a compass

9/1/07

QUILTED MEMORIES

Patterns in my life repeat like quilted memories.
Single strands of thread intertwine creating layers
Of lessons that span generations beyond my genetic
recollection.
A collective unconsciousness of low self-esteem, I
hold
Not even aware of the effects it is having on my
Un-conceived children. I don't know who I am
anymore.
I can't remember a time that I wasn't lied to, beat
down
Mentally, spiritually slaughtered.
But I remember the time I found you.
I was choking, drowning in my own tears of
hopelessness
And self hatred. I didn't first recognize you, so I
passed you by
But feeling you pass through me, was a lucid calm;
temporary but powerful
Like the eye of a hurricane.
My nonexistent boundaries left me gooey
Like silly putty melting into anyone who acted in the
least bit
Like they loved me. A chameleon- I was whatever
they were
As long as they liked me. Suppressing intuitions of
betrayal
I knew to be true, I just kept on trying to please.
Manipulated by well timed "I love you's" and "I'm
sorry's"

I failed to see that those intermittent admissions of
"truth"
Were just a fraction of the big picture.
Then I met him. He was the Him of all Hims.
It was he who would be my greatest lesson
And my bridge to reality.....as well as back to you.
Through denial and codependency, we connected.
With my eyes wide open I became lost in his maze of
trickery.
I gauged out my own eyes so I became blind to the
obvious.
It was that pattern repeating like cross-stitch, cross
roads
Bring me back to what is true. It took some months
but
I finally made it back to you. And now I see
unacceptable for what it is,
And I know that N and O are not just two
consecutive letters
In the alphabet. I am like a 2 year old learning to
stand up for myself
For the first time. No. Stand up. I fall.
And I still may not know completely who I am, but
I know who I am not. And every night when I fall to
my knees,
And every morning when I call your name in
gratitude,
I get a little piece of me in return, I get a little more
clear.
And I know that if I just keep coming back to you,
I'll be more aware. And eventually, the patterns of
my life
Once repeated will fade away into an old quilted
memory.

9/3/07

FREE WRITE #777

Age old feelings rise from the depths
Of the dead sea of my heart.
Resentments that I had long repressed
Come to haunt me. He is a totem.
A representation of all those who have
Ever told me they loved me and then
Betrayed me. Broken promises;
I never knew what grief felt like.
I mean I knew intellectually what I
Should feel like-----Elizabeth Kubler Ross
Says you experience it in five stages:
Denial, anger, bargaining, depression, acceptance;
But I never felt grief before.
I never really felt anything.
You see repression is the act of pushing
Deep down my semblance of emotion
Until the only thing you feel is numb.
So I experienced the emotion of numbness.
And perhaps the mere fact that I have denied
My feelings for so long indicates that my
Grief process probably actually started when I was
12;
The age I wrote my first poem.
I put words on paper that I wasn't supposed
To feel. Emotions were forbidden aloud
So I silently shed them through black tears
To fallen trees.
There is only so long you can stuff a trash
Can before it overflows, and when you shake
A closed carbonated drink it explodes.
And I was a ticking time bomb. My second
Stage wasn't anger, it was rage.

So, I bargain for what used to be;
Try to negotiate what I can't see;
Am I supposed to feel that crushing sensation in my
chest?
Acceptance hasn't happened yet.
Hold it together now, hold it together.
I violently erupt heaving and barely breathing,
The sounds of my tears louder than the ceramic
Elephant I threw smashing against the wall.
My life an illusion; shattered, I grieve.
Suppression no longer serves a purpose.
Awareness, acceptance and action are
My only opportunity for peace.

9/22/07

PILLOW CRIES

"Don't get emotional, it's not what I'm supposed to do
Please do not cry when a patient dies
Being rational = being professional
So swallow those tears in your eyes

"You're cold and emotionless" says the family
Who taught me not to let my eyes leak
Because wearing your emotions on your sleeve
Will ultimately make you appear weak

If I cry around women, I'm manipulative
If I cry around men, I'm dramatic
When water drips from the natural sources
On my face, society classifies me as erratic

But what happens when those choked back tears
Have no place to make their escape
Swallowed with fear, shame and the
Desire to be strong, the darkness takes its shape

Choked down, choked back, Held back Her back
Is Nailed against the wall,
Invisibly, invincibly, unrecognizably. Imposter
She lyingly stands tall

Absorbing pain from all whom she supports
Her tears fall on deaf souls
Corporate fire doesn't care about her feelings
Nor does the hope in her children's eyes

She must catch corporate daggers
Redirecting stupidity & ignorance
Then come home like she's freshly awakened
To empower her children's brilliance

All day the world says "hold your tears queen"
Teaching her to suppress herself emotionally
But in the quiet of the night, there the tears go
To the only place that will accept them without
judgment and willingly

4/6/18

FREEDOM

Is this what it feels like to be free?
I'm floating like clouds
With clouds
Gazing at khaki and green mosaics below me.
Mixing with the heavens and the hum of
A 767, I close my eyes.
The space fills my being with vibrations
That reverberate to the bone.
OMMM
We move a thousand miles an hour
Yet I am perfectly still.
Give me life in slow motion as I travel back in time.

Is this what it feels like to be free?
I am floating like yogis
With yogis
Taking in deeper breaths with each inhale.
The prana moves to my hips as they lift almost
Effortlessly. Floating back to Chaturanga
I take upward dog.......
then downward dog.
I become invisible like the atmosphere
I breathe, my form dissolving into
Nothingness
Give me life in slow motion as I travel back in time.

Is this what it feels like to be free?
I'm floating like music
With music
The notes circling my crown like halos.
Children of Mali lead me through a land

I've never seen
Then Congo and Cuba unite to
Harmonizing percussions and string and horn
So I do a little salsa step.
Then the call of North African drums beckons me
my hips follow the pattern of a figure eight
and I let my shoulders shimmy
Give me life in slow motion as I travel back in time

Is this what it feels like to be free?
I'm floating like freedom
With freedom
Maintaining presence in every moment
I kiss souls in heaven while I
Dance with los ninos de Peru.
I float in lotus while spitting
Invocations with Pattabi Jois
Life passes us every day at the
Speed of light. The world is
Constantly spinning in
Fast forward.
But give me life in slow motion
Or even rewind
Give me life in slow motion as I travel back in time.
MTC 10/06

UNTITLED

*I want to be like a cool flowing stream in the winter
time,*
Brisk and unafraid of the path that lies before me.
Traveling vigorously to my unknown destination,
Expanding and Contracting to degrees Celsius.
Solidifying and melting on the sun's command.
Running smoothly over jagged edges.
*I want to be like a cool flowing stream in the
springtime*
Soft and refreshing, bathing all forms of life in
My love and purity.
Cascading
> *And*
>> *Cascading*
>>> *And*
>>>> *Cascading until*
I reach a calm quiet stroll
Uniting with my fellow hydrogen and oxygen
brothers and sisters.
I want to go with the flow
I want to go where they flow.
*I want to be like a cool flowing stream in the
summertime*
Patiently waiting to hold hands with children,
I want to tickle their feet and hear their laughter,
*I want to comfort and rejuvenate those who make
ripples in my soul*
*My spirit bubbles. I want to be a mirror reflecting the
beauty in all*
Who dare to see, I want to reflect the beauty in me.
*I want to be a cool flowing stream in autumn soaking
up*

Red, yellow, and orange leaves as they fall trickling
One by one, freedom floating creating hyperboles
Until gently connecting with rushing water, creating
Rafts for nearby 6 legged gypsies.
I want to be a cool flowing stream.
I want to be a cool flowing stream in springtime.
But instead, I am just afraid.

MTC 01/2007

REBORN

It's funny...I had visualized this day
A thousand times---
Driving, car in front—can't stop—
Lose control---sudden darkness---
A spiritual blackout and all I can hear
Is the sound of my own breath.
Tick tock--- time slows my heart,
And it doesn't hurt, it doesn't feel,
And it isn't like I thought it would be
Because I realized suddenly that
I'm not as ready as I once was to lose
consciousness.
Still have too much life to live
Still have too much healing to give.
Now my mind is spinning...
Is that metallic taste the
taste of my own regret, the
taste of all the things I haven't done yet?
Or is it just the taste of my own blood
Draining the life out of my body----
Now spinning---- is that my life
Flashing before my eyes, or is it my future,
Perhaps it's just a hallucination as the
Oxygen in my brain begins to dwindle.
Suddenly sirens, yelling, pulling...
Pulling me out of my body and
I don't want to go, but it feels so right,
It just feels so light-----
Please shield my eyes, the sun's too bright!
And a man yells
"Clear!"

"Charging 360,
 Clear!"
"Charging, Again, 360!"
"Clear!
And I am ---- clear
And Free to be
Reborn.

3/13/10

METAPHYSICSPIRITUAL

CHAOS

Chaos is an indicator of transformation
When storm clouds darken the sky
Threatening to wash away the soil in
Which our seeds of hope were planted...
When lightning makes dangerous the
Very earth that grounds us, and
Thunder deafens us to the whispers of God's voice
We are blinded to our own possibility
But blindness can bring blessings
Creating doors to the infinite.
Scientists say that when one sense is
Taken away the others are heightened.
I imagine it's like the newness of well water
The day Helen Keller realized she could
Talk with her hands.
Where is your well?
Are you still focused on what's wrong or
Can you find peace in the eye of the storm?
Stay there...move with it....be still,
And know that it is God.

Change happens by default but
Transformation is a choice, and the
Opportunity is not to be determined
By your circumstance, but to be empowered
By your choices
Live not by the whim of your identity but
By the strength of your word
Because your "Word is bond"
Yeah, that's not just an old outdated saying,
It's what distinguishes those with integrity and
power

From the victims of life
Live like it has power
Remember your lives as King & Queens
You used to create with simply the power of
Your word. Wake Up, Now and remember
yourselves.
Nothing has changed except the scenery.
We are still royalty, powerful and creative
Limited only by our view and unwillingness to
Take 100% responsibility for the impact we have on
The future of humanity. And it begins
With what we create for ourselves...in word
We can choose to be blind to the future
Be deaf to hope
Be mute to our own inspiration, but
Let's not be numb...
Not to this chaos
Because chaos is an indicator, and it's
Only after our life has been turned upside down
In our rearview mirror that we recognize
That the rainbow was always there waiting for us
On the other side...

6/7/16 (modified 4/3/18)

THE SECRET

You think and therefore you are.
Do you believe?
Do you know the power,
The quantum influence in one single thought?
Did you know that every consideration in your
Conscious and subconscious manifest
Which each passing moment created
By you and in you?
The law of attraction.

You see I am a healer, one that
Did not arrive by clever nature alone
But by inventive imagination.
I conceived each instant
Each moment walking the path
That lay before me.
Even though I have worked
Overtime for two letters
That seemed so much more important
Five years ago, than they are to me now,
I tremble with gratitude for the gift
That I am given.
I create the vision,
Let it envelop me
Digesting, absorbing it daily.

And you...
Your words have more power than
A nuclear detonator
They are a karmic sound wave that
Resonates truth, creating your very reality.

But are you a believer?
Do you create or do you destroy?
Do you worship the struggle or
Thank God for the gift?

To reside in negativity only gives it power.
Our war on terror, breeds more terrorists
Our war on drugs, creates addicts and dealers.
As we fight world hunger, we generate more mouths
to feed.
That on which we dwell, we energetically enforce.
Why? Because the universe does not distinguish
desire from
Disgust it only picks up the energy from the thoughts
That we release.

We are reverberating beings of light
And the universe is our genie.
Every thought we produce sends out
A silent thunderclap into the universe
And our Maker responds,
"Your wish, is my command"

So if you are anti-war, be pro peace
If you are anti-drugs, be pro clean
If you are anti-SUV be pro Toyota Corolla
And if you are anti-me, be pro you.
Because we are made in the image and
Likeness of God, and God is the ultimate Creator

So I will meet you
In the back of your mind, and I
Will come equipped with mine because
We are all in the House of the Divine, and our
Minds are a most powerful (or the most dangerous)
Place to be.

MY REBIRTH

God told me that I was going to die last night
He said that my life would no longer be
By tomorrow at a quarter past three
And so I began to prepare judiciously for my exit.
18 hours is not long enough to let everyone know
how
much you love them, but I sat down with my
address book determined that I was going to get
it done no matter how long it took (at long as it
was under 18 hours). First, I called my mother
then of course my dad. My cousin Enike, Aisha
and then my aunt val.
How was I supposed to give such news to my little
sister?
But I called her anyway and told her how much
I'd miss her. Sparing you the details of what took
Me all night, I went through my book calling until
Early daylight. My mother hopped in her 4runner
And was at the front door by dawn, my dad hopped
the first flight out, by eight he showed up on my
lawn.
The whole family at my place, my friends coming by
I felt so at peace with them there only hours before
I was to die.
But at two forty five I begged them to depart. I
wanted
The last 15 minutes alone to cuddle with my heart
I called the man downstairs and he held on to me
tight.
Together we began to pray we knew it'd be alright
God told me the other night that I was to die at 3

87

*But there was one small detail that he neglected to
tell me.
When three arrived and I was still here I felt like
I'd been forlorn. But what I didn't realize
Is that I had been reborn.
What I had just experienced, a miracle of god's grace
A chance to live life differently to take it at God's
pace.
With the rebirth of my soul and a different point of
view
I took to life God's truth in mind.*

REPRESENTATIONS OF GOD

I am only unaccepted in acceptable places
And I am recognized in unrecognizable spaces
I hide behind my mind but I'm
Exploited by my words
If I didn't meditate daily
I'd float away with the birds
I converse with God best while
Sitting under a tree, and many
Can reach God by conversating with me.
My heart bleeds many cultures but
Most see me as just one
Rising from Dominican mountains
I set as the New Zealand sun
In Arabic, I am called friend
And in Swahili I am life
In my past life, I was her husband
And in this one I am his wife.
I was born when the trees pushed
The earth from the sky.
The wind whispered my presence
In God's invisible sigh
I am an elder reborn
A newborn reincarnated.
Through the many wombs of Yahweh
I have been transmigrated
You and I began together
As an unnamed irony
The earth flows through our veins
Revealing that you and I are really we
Convoluted exploitations, history
Cannot be undone

Connecting centuries in seconds
Exposes that we are really one
Still you survey my intentions
Attempting to understand
Scrutinizing me as if I am
Some kind of complex cryptogram
My eyes reflect your eyes with
Certain underlying doubt
You fuse your soul to mine
Now grasping what it's all about
A speculative journey
You now realize our façade
I represent you, and you
Represent God.

MTC 12/26/06

THE TREE

She looked up and said "God I want to be free,
please take my world my will from me"

I replied, "child be like that tree
Swaying with the breeze so carelessly."

"But the wind is harsh, God I don't feel strong"

"My child, surrender, let it carry you on.
The leaves don't fight as crosswinds blow.
They embrace its strength and just let go.

"but I'm afraid of what I can't see"

"Then put your unwavering trust in me.
Look at that tree, she has no fear. Through many
Trials she still stands here. She's not put off
By tornadoes past, nor does she fall to future
Forecast. She doesn't obsess about what could be
Lightning doesn't cause her to flee. She just remains
In the moment gratefully, surrendering to the
elements
Effortlessly."

With tears, she replied, "But my thoughts don't yield
And I honestly don't know what's false and what's
real.
My daily obsessions cause me to fret. I act on what
hasn't
Even happened yet!"

I look at my child seeing all of her doubt. It was time
To show her a different route. All of her fears, I allowed
To come true. I observe now what she'd next choose to do.
Angrily, she called out my name, "God why'd you forsake me?"
She cried out in blame.

"My child," I said, "take a look around. You'll find your feet still
stand on the ground. The earth is still turning you did not implode.
Your heart is still beating, it did not explode.   Now look through
The window, child, what do you see?"
With tears in her eyes she looked at the tree.

"See child, you must keep your belief strong like her roots,
you must make your faith unwavering and absolute.
Stand straight and strong with thickened skin,
But hold compassion and knowledge within.
Let your arms outstretch inviting all in your heart
But let no succubus tear you apart.
You must tremble in appreciation for the breeze
And let harsh weather flow through you
With fearless ease.
Dance to the music of falling rain
Be vulnerable enough to show your pain.
Do not blink to lightning in the sky.
And don't let thunder make you cry.
In quiet nights meditate and be still
When the hurricane comes, embrace the thrill.
Be audacious to man's chainsaw
And of my beauty, you stand in awe.

92

Remain humble yet potent, stand firm and tall
But know that I will catch you when you fall."

With great resolve she drew a breath,
Ready to lay her will to rest.
With surrender came tranquility, a
Peacefully equanimity.
She finally whispered, with a quiet woe
I can't, you can, God I think I'll let go.

5/6/07

TWELVE MONTHS OF FOREVER

Happy.
Happiness is a fantasy that I thought only
Existed in pixels and projections.
Perplexing that I was never privy.
I played with praise, pretending
To be appeased
All the while I was plunging;
Plunging painfully into
Paroxysmal self-pity
I was a perpetrator,
A paradoxical participant.
But what I soon came to see
Was that I had sacrificed
My serenity for senseless
Solicitude, self-deprivation,
And isolation.
I had self-sabotaged my own safety
In co-dependence.
So sordid was my self-esteem
It shocked me, shook me,
To find that I was so unhappy.

New
New life comes nearly one year later.
And nestled in this newfangled
Nakedness of emotion, I am free.
I nap in the naivety of namelessness
And nourishment, as I narrate
A new ending to this nebulous hereafter.
And Thereafter, I abandon
Abomination, aberration, and abasement.

I apply acceptance.
And the actualization accentuates
My appreciation so much that I
Become an accessory to love.
Leaving behind accumulations
Of unacceptable operations
That lead to admonishing accusations.
Instead I opt for awareness and adoration.
I know that in adversity I can sometimes
Be my own adversary, so I choose a different
Occupation...an unfamiliar avenue.

Year
Years of my life departed have
Left me yearning. Yen and
Yellow-bellied, the youthfulness
Of yesterday has failed me. Yoked me.
And in fear, I have yielded, yelling
Silent boundaries yet letting "yes"
Slip from my lips constantly.
But this year breeds breakthroughs;
And I break out of bondage and
Become born again.
Not merely because of a faith
That I uphold, because of the
Beauty I bestow.
I am the beneficiary and
The benefactor of so many
Blessings before me.
Leaving so much bitterness behind me.
I am no longer a bystander to bravery.
I am a beginner again,
and as I begin again I brainstorm
benedictions of betterment;
believing that beauty begets beauty

95

and I become that which I behold.

And the happiness that I refused
To harbor previously has now
Harmoniously settled within me.
The heavy hue of past hurt, now
Becomes a distant glow providing
Healing to my soul.
Now heightened, humbled, and hushed,
I sit here...inaugurated into another
Twelve months of forever
And challenged to live
One day at a time.

1/1/08

RANDOM THOUGHTS

Amoeba shapes crawl on my wall;
It's 12:16 am;
Making lists of things to do;
Hallucinating shadows over my bed;
Walk barefoot on sandpaper;
Fetching mail from a week ago;
Speckled white hints spring
outside my bathroom window;
I fantasize about the day he
Actually says "I love you"
Why hasn't he called yet?
Oh, it's only been 12 hours.
I am spinning faster than my ceiling fan.
I contemplate if I will actually
Get up for yoga tomorrow since
I am still up writing this poem when
I am supposed to be sleeping.
It's the same excuse every night.
This night shirt is too hot, but
I just may be too lazy to get up and change it....
Or maybe not.
I notice I'm getting hives;
What am I allergic to?
The texture of my skin is so silky.
How can anyone NOT want to touch – I do.
I'm thirsty...
I need to call my Dad..
I need to call Tia V...
I need to call a lot of people!
No obligation next weekend
Giving myself permission to just BE

Why am I still up?
I've got to get up at 6:30 in the morning.
I guess tomorrow won't be a yoga morning after all.
This is all so random.
I wonder when this will turn into a poem.

5/26/09

UNTITLED

If I had it all my way,
I'd be a billion pixels on a million screens
Creating fires inside the souls
Whose eyes land upon my lips.
Sparking life like jumper cables
on dead batteries.
Creating movement of mindset
And bodies of breakthroughs.
If I had it all my way.

If the world was my oyster
I'd wake up to white sand;
Sing silence to the morning
On my mat, salutations to the sun
And awakening the body.
I'd retreat for days with 20 of my kin;
Kindred with transformation in mind
New perspectives and guidance
Begets healing and prosperity
If the world was my oyster.

If I had a magic wand,
I'd travel the world facilitating
Greatness in others.
I'd stand for love, generating
passion amongst droves.
I'd speak to thousands at a time,
Inspiring thirsty hearts,
Unlocking mighty souls,
Empowering lost spirits,
If I had a magic wand.

If the world were according to my say
I'd fall asleep
In the arms of my king,
Kissed on the forehead. After
kissing our two young ones to bed;
I'd be grateful and secure that
When I open my eyes upon sunrise
He'd still be there---waiting
To give me the world in a day, everyday
If the world were according to my say.

If my integrity ruled the earth
I'd spread love, and earn money
In my sleep.
Financial freedom married to transparency,
My intention remains unobscured
By my wealth.
Endless and effortless income
Allowing for continuous
Unencumbered contribution.
If my integrity ruled the earth.

If I were completely awake,
I'd see that Life is already perfect, &
that imperfections are beautiful.
The world is chaotic, and
In perfect order, and
All things occur in Divine timing,
And time is a dream that we create.
See if I were completely awake,
I'd recognize that thoughts are controllable
And word is powerful;
That action is key, and faith
Will become the eyes that guide me.

When I am completely awake,
I see that the world is already my oyster,
And the magic wand is on the
Tip of my tongue.
Because what I say, I manifest.
And I am my word,
And my word becomes my integrity,
And my integrity rules my earth.
So the truth is, I already have my say, and
The world is already going my way.
I just must have the courage to continue
To create it, with presence.

01/16/12

THE PEACE WE WISH TO HAVE

Jacksonville Earth

Breathe the salt water air
Into my soul, take me in
Through large and small bronchioles.
The freshness of the oxygen
Diffuses into my capillaries
Bringing the spirit new vitality.
I share energies with the Spanish moss
That travels with the wind like
Dental floss
clinging to trees becoming lost
in absorbing peaceful equanimity
With nothing but the sound of
Singing locusts quietly.
In the background crickets
Chirp and to the music the
 Fire ants Work
Building houses judiciously
Until they become suddenly aware of me.
Then they gather 'round my toes
Wondering what I'm about
To bestow. Wondering what this
Giant means corrupting their
Precious green.
I send the subliminal that
I intend no flaw
But of God's orchestra
I am in awe.
A natural refuge for peace
A medium for creative release
Invocations roll from my tongue
As I breathe Her presence into my lungs
I become the macrocosm

103

with which I seek to coalesce,
The eternal Divinity within

MTC 8/26/06

UNTITLED

*Sun kisses the sky as the moon hides jealously in
plain sight
Waiting to be seen; wishing the horizon will hurry up
and
Swallow the sun; Moon thinks "how can I move
time?
Then move time again so that I never have to be
invisible.
Maybe I can rise the tides high enough to put the
sun's fire out,
Or maybe I can convince the horizon to hold the sun
down
When the morning comes. I could even cohort with
the clouds
To unite and form a fortress so that the sun's rays
are muted,
And even during the daylight hours I can be seen in
all my glory"
As he schemed and strategized, the sun he chastises
Passing with a fake smile and a "hello"
Silently smirking at what the sun fails to know;
Cordially greeting her with a contemptuous smile.
Killing her off in the back of his mind all the while.
After 30 empty days and 29 meaningless nights
Miserable moon had an idea to strike.
He would distract the sun on their morning meet
mid-sky
With conversation so sweet that the sun would forget
to rise,
Then the moon would have to itself the skies.
He rejoiced in his plan "Finally"!!! He thought
So he waited for the morning unabatedly, and*

105

As the sun rose, the moon deviously stopped the sun
And asked, "What is it like Sun? To light up the sky,
To make people so happy as you pass them by?"
The sun stopped surprised and in a thoughtful way,
(And the moon thought "Yes, I'll have my way!")
Then over the sun comes with sadness in her eyes,
And says "It's quite wonderful but I wish I could rise
And illuminate the stars as you do,
Bringing romance and beauty with your perfect hue.
A voice to the stars and peace to the soul
Sleep to you and wake up feeling whole.
I may light up the sky so that people can see,
But your light allows people's hearts to be free
Your power controls the ocean's tides, In your
phases fertility resides
And the worst, moon is we don't get to play
Since we only pass briefly twice a day"
The moon hung his head with tears in his eyes
The sun appeared puzzled, "Moon why do you cry?"
With shame in his voice as he looked away,
"Sun I had no idea that you felt this way.
I was so consumed in jealousy,
I missed the blessing that I could be.
In missing the difference I could make,
I get the impact that's at stake.
The romances that go unborn,
The waiting souls that then would mourn.
In the selfishness of my envy,
Why would you want to play with me?"
Sun smiled gently, the Moon blushed more
"Together massive impacts we'll implore
What we see as fallible to others is quite invaluable
Like our eclipse, look at the awe of how
Our union defies law."
With that, the moon could gratefully see
How Sun had truly set him free.

And who could imagine that all of this could
Go on as we look upon what appears to be
A simple solar Eclipse.

7/2015

UNTITLED

Sky-kissed ocean looks like paradise.
Turquois teal transforms to foaming cloud
When the crest communicates that it
Can no longer hold its perfect shape.
Forming majestic waves with fierce and
Unsuspecting undercurrents that rip apart
The most stable stance.
Waves meet rocking roughness with power
Shaping the mountain ever so slightly
With each communication.

And who are we?
Who are we but beautiful crests
Holding our form until we can no longer;
Crashing violently into those with
Seemingly solid stance;
Turning lives upside down or
Shaping slightly with each touch.
From afar it seems like paradise to another,
Yet with each successive wave, we are
Fighting for our lives.
We are sun-kissed with an infinite forever
And our backs are turned to the horizon,
Too busy surviving the last wave, and anticipating
the next.
We are sun kissed with an infinite forever, and our
Feet are buried in the sand in attempt to
Ground us in what we'd call "reality" and
What others might call irony.

How can we reach what we can't see
that we can't see?

For if we surrender we may be
Cast into blind breathlessness
Uncontrollably fading away into nothing.
And what if we were nothing, and not afraid?
What if we embraced the blind breathlessness
That sweeps us through the unknown—
The uncontrolled
The free.
Death begets new birth, and
The unknown begets limitless pathways.
The ocean of life is vast, deep, and endless
And to experience the eternal,
we must be brave enough to turn around.

7/20/14

I DON'T KNOW WHAT TO SAY

I don't know anymore what to say.
I simply rise with the sun each day
To pay homage to the Manduka black mat
Singing "mo ha Shanti 'ay"
I salute the sun with gratitude
Letting my breath adjust my attitude
Approximately one hundred five minutes of stillness
And sweaty slow bends
and extends as the steady flow within
prepares me for the challenges of the day
and I still don't really know what to say.

I'm entering the chase and plugging in.
Another day of my assignment begins
As energies in need come seeking my view
I let God guide the proper message through
My mouth often says what I need to hear,
And though messages seem to come so clear
I wonder to them am I making sense
I'm here to pay forward a positive difference
I need a hand to guide my way,
Because I simply don't know what to say.

Line after line black words on the screen
An infinite space travels wisdom between
Their desktops, laptops, tablets, smartphones,
I wonder the reach of my words from this home.
I look at my insights, I look at my new likes
I analyze analytics to see what I must fix
To impact more tomorrow than I did to day,
And I still don't know what I'm supposed to say.

Events of the day swirl inside my head
I ponder all the things I've done and said
The message I've shared, the things I've taught
The inspiration & empowerment brought
Unsure where things come from or where I begin
But in the right moments the right words rush in.
It seems to always work out that way
When I ignore what I think I'm supposed to say.

Words that show up are just like syllables combined.
My intentions allow access to the Divine
The actions that show up day after day,
The letting my spirit show me the way.
The knowing I don't have to always know,
That impact is in the love that I show.
That everything I do creates a ripple,
My charge is to keep the message simple.
And really at the end of the day,
It doesn't really matter what I say.
It only matters who I be
and who is listening....

5/15/11

Dr. Maiysha Clairborne

THE FACES WE DON'T SEE

I be --- a part of we
Bearing fruit from collective tree
Sharing of blood and ancestry

I be --- a part of we
Graduate university
For a career in community

I be --- a part of we
Nurturing wife and mother of three
Runs business simultaneously

I be --- a part of we
Speak truth with no uncertainty
Fights through her insecurity

I be --- a part of we
Survive the husband beating me
Go on to thrive successfully

I be --- a part of we
That shall make no apology
In face of our adversity

I be --- a part of we
That despite her anxiety
Chooses to live life authentically

I be --- a part of we
Commit and care devotedly
For sick and dying family

I be --- a part of we
Walk away from malignancy
Towards her spirituality

I be --- a part of we
Creates what others can't for-see
Achieves things to her own degree

I be --- a part of we
Embrace our own complexity
Turn away from complacency

I be --- a part of we
With wavering consistency
Continue self-discovery

I be --- a part of we
Handling road blocks skillfully
And with a great humility

I be --- a part of we
Regardless of propaganda she
Maintains her own identity

I be --- a part of we
A Face that no one ever sees
Safe in her anonymity
A form of great diversity

I be --- a part of we
Sharing wonderful history
Bearing fruit from collective tree
I be

5/20/10

SECOND CHANCES

There is this point just before the waves crash
When the sunlight sparkles on the crest as if it's
About to wash a thousand diamonds to shore.
That is my light at the end of the tunnel.
Watch crystal salt water carry knife-like pieces
Of dead coral to the surface and then--take it away
again;
Repeating reminders of suffering---meanwhile
Lost schools of fish, desperate for attention,
Swim closely to the shore waiting on their
Large white giants with plastic masks and
Various colored body wear to look upon them again.
It's like they choose to be in an aquarium.
At a sandbar not an hour's boat ride away swim
At least a dozen stingray families.
They only have Fridays off for the rest of the week
Is spent earning their keep as part of the tourist
Industry---allowing hundreds of foreign fingers
To feel silk smooth skin, involuntarily massaging
backs;
Like sea prostitutes, they are pimped out receiving
a handful of squid for their troubles.
I was told that actually they don't like to be held,
but they do it to please their masters.
And how many people don't like to be held---
Held to do things that are counterintuitive and
Invasive to their very nature, but they do it anyway--
-
To put food on the table---to put children through
school---
To give a life --- better than they grew up with.
A passionless existence, I see the world living in

*Black and white re-runs, leave "Life" packed up in
the attic
Like an old fading memory---forget what fun even
looks like—
Just driving back and forth to work
Eighteen hours at a time until we collapse and die
At thirty-seven of a disease that we should not have
Killed us until seventy-nine----
until we have cancers growing in our breasts,
ulcers growing through our stomachs, and
plaques closing up our arteries --- we are killing
ourselves.
Because irreversible mutations cause constant
irritation
To every single cell in our body causing Dis-Ease.
Our tolerance for the unacceptable is too high.
We take one week out of every fifty-two for vacation,
And I am guilty, work twelve hour days and call
internet
Rest, and I am guilty, but sitting in front of crystal
crashing
Waves restores my sanity.
Dead corals in stead of diamonds remind me that
Suffering is optional, and if I want to break patterns,
Then I must break patterns---
So I run to the sparkling blue messiah and submit,
Baptizing myself. Today I wash away my sins of
Self neglect, self-sabotage, and self-abandonment,
Replace it with self awareness, self-love, and self
care.
I re-emerge into life as a newborn, ready
To experience life, with presence
5/20/10*

LEAN IN

I am powerless over my first thought,
But I'm not powerless over the second.
I feel the tailspin in my brain that comes
With the burn in my stomach when my mind
Becomes topsy turvy with thoughts of things
That I swear I can control if I just
Worry......a little......harder....
But the obsession only leads to
Further frustration, and I realize at that moment
That to make it go away I have to stop fighting
And so I lean in.

I had to call a healthy friend today,
And didn't have a clue what to say, because
My mental was on lock like
Broken records repeating past lies
That run through my veins and
Straight to my brain .....
replacing the oxygen.
So she came to my rescue,
To rip me away from the carousel
Of crazy. Where reality was the result and
The truth is that it was like ice picks
In my eyes, so they welled up in
Surprise and I leaned in.

I was reminded the other day that
No matter how far I've come,
There I can still go...and crazy
Is just around the corner...doing
Push ups in the parking lot, playing

My perceptions on the turn table
Of warped obsession,
contained in a negative pressure room.
And when I unlock the deadbolt
And let isolation escape me, the
Blood rushes to my head along with
The relief that is sound mind, and
My reality does not always represent
The actuality, so I lean in.

It's time to put my big girl panties on
Now, and speak up for my wants and needs.
For lifetimes I have stifled for the sake of
Saved conflict and avoidance of abandonment,
But at the cost of contentment, and
With the price of contempt. So, I
Ask the questions, and I speak the
Necessary, then I wait for the
Reciprocal response that lets
Me know that God is listening and
That it is okay for me to
Lean in.

I find life a series of opportunities
To be present, a collection of moments
That lead us to now.
And no matter how fast we run,
or how far we go, we always end up
Where we are...which is here. Here...
Where Realities are not always congruent
And actualities take you through it,
But we have choices...the choice to
Wake up, and escape our fantasy,
The choice to wake up and activate
Plan B-E.
It's all we have to do, when we

117

Get short of breath, it's all we have
To do when we feel that pain in our chest,
So, Just when you feel like you are about
To pass out from the light, resist the urge
To Resist LIFE, just ......just
LEAN IN!

6/ 12/ 09

One-Way Argument with God

I'm having a one-way argument with God,
And I'm asking him for confirmation that he's here,
When so many things in my life seem
Up in the air, like where is last weeks' money today
And why aren't things really going my way.
Is mercury still in retrograde or is my attitude just
gray.
So, I'm having a conversation with God

I'm having a one-way argument with God because
Last week there seemed to be a hole in my bank
account.
And while that is speculation what wasn't
imagination
Was the nail in my tire and the same week my
circuit breaker
In the house goes haywire, then I call for repair and
my
Home warranty's expired, I'm in job transition so
financial
Situation is dire, so I'm having this conversation with
God

I'm having a one-way argument with God and I'm
Trying to figure out what this new relationship I'm in
is
All about. This man is amazing without a doubt, but
He's been scorned so his energy's conflicted and his
heart

Is torn, and my emotions because of this are worn,
and
I'm having this dialogue because I want to hang in,
To be compassionate of where we've both been----
I know we both want this deep within,
So I'm having this conversation with God

See, I'm having this conversation with God.
The argument is over so we dialogue; more like
I shut up and my ears unclog.
I can hear what She's been saying all along...
"The things you seek are on their way
Just trust, have faith, live in today
If you focus on what is dire
You'll manifest what you Don't desire
Be cognizant of blessings small
And be appreciative of blessings All
Just keep doing the next right thing
And watch the abundance that it brings
Accept your man and let him be
And if it's meant you'll have the key
You've both been hurt so take it slow
Let honesty and patience help you grow
And when my will has deemed so
You won't worry or ask, you'll just know
But most of all please try to see
That you'll never win an argument with me"

So I had this conversation with God
And he taught me that nothing comes with certainty,
And if I just put my faith and trust in We
The result is my ultimate serenity.
Call them arguments, dialogues, soliloquies
I keep having them...having these
Conversations with God
2/1/09

HOW LIFE OCCURS TO US....

BREATHE

The alarm clock sounds at 6am and my
Half wake arm reaches for salvation under the
Pillow as Beats Antique fills my ears.
Finger on the trigger I squeeze and silence!
The music stops, I turn over and
Breathe
Ten minutes later the beats resume.
I realize as the dawn light peaks through my
Wooden protectors that another day has
Officially arrived. Through my
still foggy consciousness,
I roll over, thank God, I open my eyes
Absorbing the sun and I
Breathe
The morning ritual is set.
Brush teeth, wash face,
Sit in front of my space heater
And strategically put on each article
Of clothing. To the kitchen,
Water on the stove, oats in the water,
Spinach, carrots, apple on counter
Waiting to be masticated.
Tea cup, water boiling, tea bag waiting.
Lunch in Tupperware, juice in cup
Cup to mouth, oats done, breakfast
On the run, grab my bag
Out of the house, wait...
Check for keys...in the pocket
Get to the car, turn the ignition and
Breathe
Music bumping I drive 85, go the back
Way, sun in my eyes,

Weaving in and out of line at
Just the right time..
Miss the light
Make the light
Trying to time it just right
Now turning into the parking lot
My income source
In anticipation of what's to come I
Breathe
The day is a blur of strangers and
Salutations, they see me I hear them,
Take a deep breath,
Here's my recommendations,
here's your prescription
Have a nice day.
In and out, twenty-two times
Washing hands like obsessive
Compulsive disorder I am
Ducking coughs and sore throats
Wearing gloves so as not to catch
fingerprints of the flu...fighting
time until three quarters past five
wash my hands one more time and I
Breathe

Back to my car,
Plug my musical God into
The cable that sends serendipity
To my ears. Start the car,
Start to sing, start to feel hungry.
My stomach and I have conversations
Of how we will satisfy each other
When I arrive home.
Pull in the driveway and initiate
Evening ritual.

No... kids first..
No time for me...
Dinner is served
then upstairs
Space heater on
Kids in bath
Clothes on bed,
Tea on stove
Computer on lap
Surf on net
Charts, Charts, Charts
Watch my shows (maybe)
Eat my cold food
That I was supposed to eat
Earlier
The night is done
Bedtime comes
I turn my electric blanket on,
Create darkness just before
Slipping into my comfortable
Haven of heaven.
My mind drifts toward delta waves
And before I let go, I thank God
For the day and I
Breathe

11/8/08

SMOKE SCREEN

Life is a smoke screen created by our own
Imagination of truth.
Today I woke up this morning
Grateful as with every day and
Hopeful of what dreams may be
Realized, only to have my emotions
Misted by one thought that hadn't even
Happened yet.....cue foggy mind.
Smoke screen...
When you're helping people,
and life makes sense... then it doesn't..
my thirty-two year old med school
classmate found dead, brains scattered
on the walls, by his own hand. And found
by his unsuspecting girlfriend....
Aren't we all unsuspecting...
Smoke screen....
When your best friend gets the good news
That she is breast cancer free exactly
One year and three months to the day
That her husband survived a blood vessel
Bursting in his closed cranium...
Your eyes well with joy...then with
Sadness from the next call that reveals
That your sister in law to be has just been
Diagnosed with a more aggressive breast cancer...
Than the one that your friend survives...
And she is only 31.
Smoke screen
When you work 10 hour days, putting
Money away...building your nest egg
With hope and intention, knowing it's

125

Taken years for you to get to this
Place of financial stability and
Security, and just when
You are about to pay that last
Credit card off and become debt free...
The flood robs you of that
Serenity.
Smoke screen
I walk blinded by the cool mist
That clouds my way leading me
Through unexpected mazes----
Dreams that I wish to wake up from.
And sometimes I see rays of light
And feel the warmth from the sun---
Remind me, God of why I'm here
And where I come from-----
I was told my calling was to help others,
But the smoke keeps my visibility
Limited, and I get in my own way
When I keep believing that I can
Fix the machine creating the smoke:
"What an illusion!" God said
Question mark over my head.
So, She told me that my job is to
walk through the smoke
Grabbing hands along the way---
Their cold hands; my warm heart;
We are still blind and life is still
A smoke screen, but
If I just keep walking forward,
dauntless and unyielding, the
Smoke will clear to reveal
That I was never alone

11/28/09

THIS SHIT REALLY HAPPENS

Good morning, I'm Dr.Life. How can I help you today?

"Well doc, I've had this cough for a day and what I really need

for you to do is to write me for some Penicillin because every time

I get a cough it always goes to my chest, and I was reading on WEBMD

That it is probably bronchitis so if you'd kindly give me a script, I'll

Just be on my way to take care of my cough that I've just had for a day"

Good morning, I'm Dr. Life. How may I help you today?

"ummmmm, doctor I've got a headache and I was wondering if I could

get a scan of my brain....and I know you'll think this is totally insane,

but my friend was watching Access Hollywood and they said that

young people with headaches could have brain tumors. And even though

I've only had the headache twice, and two Advil for the pain did suffice,

After consulting the internet we both agree that it's just the best option...

Just to be safe...and I'll need a referral to Neurology too."

Good morning, I'm Dr. Life. How may I help you today?

"Yes doc, I was reading on the internet about this new medication

that makes your eyelashes grow longer and stronger.

Then of course when I saw that Brooke Shields uses it, I knew

It must be for me." "Well, ma'am but your eyelashes look fine,

And these meds come with potential side effects"

"Doc, I don't care about the potential problems it may cause, I just want

longer lashes so I can look hot....and since it's not covered by

my insurance, I was wondering...you got any samples?"

Good morning, I'm Dr. Life. How may I help you today?

"Doc...my hemorrhoids...they're killing me......"

Sigh!

Good morning, I'm Dr. Life. How can I help you today?

"Oh, I just need a work excuse for the last 3 days"

"Okay, what seems to be the problem?"

" Well, ummmm, I wasn't feeling well..."

"Okay, what were your symptoms?"

"I...just wasn't feeling good...I was tired and I had...a

ummmm...cough...and a ...headache"

"Well, alright, I'll just put slackeritis on the excuse,
will that do?"

Good morning, I'm Dr. Life. How may I help you
today?
"Oh hey sweet darlin' I'm just here for my
Viagra. You see
I've got this new girlfriend in the assisted
living facility, and things are
Getting pretty serious with her and me. I'm
planning a little
Rendezvous in room 302, after the senior
dance this weekend."
"Well, sir it's nice to know sex still exists after
80...now do you
have any medical problems?" "No, just my
hearing...are you the
doctor?" Yes, sir...here is your script for the
Viagra. Don't break
a hip, now okay?" "Okay, When's the doctor
coming in?" "I am the doctor"

Good morning, I'm doctor Life. How may I help you
today?
"You're the doctor?"
"No, I just play one on TV"

Good morning, I'm doctor Life. How may I help you
today?
"Doc, I need an orthopedic referral for shoulder
pain"
"Okay ma'am, tell me what the problem is"
Well, I have excruciating pain, when I twist
My arm back and lift it up...like...this...."

"Okay, maybe you should just STOP DOING THAT!"

Good morning, I'm doctor Life, How may I help you today?
        "Well, doctor, I have this stomach pain for the past
        3 days, and I'm sure that I have stomach cancer"
        "Okay, have you been evaluated for this before?" No
        "Okay, have you even had this before?" "No"
        "Are you vomiting blood?" "No"
        "Are you having any change in your bowel patterns?" "No"
        "Do you have a family history of stomach or intestinal cancer?" "Well, No"
        "What may I ask makes you feel so certain that you have stomach cancer?"
        "Well, I read it on WebMD of course"
        "Oh! Well, better call the family then...."

Good morning, I'm Dr. Life, How may I help you today?
        "Doc, I've got the swine flu!"
        "No, you don't"
        "Well, I've at least got Strep throat!"
        "You don't even have a fever!"
        "I never run a fever....my normal temperature is 95 degrees...98 F is high for me"
        "Ma'am if your normal temperature was 95 degrees, you'd be dead....
        Now, go home, and drink some orange juice...come back and see me
        When you are actually sick!" "You can check WebMD for the proper

Symptoms"

Good morning, I'm Dr. Life, How may I help you
today?
     "Doc, I......"
     "No...wait, let me guess...WebMD sent you------
--How
     about I just give you a prescription now for
your full body
     CT scan, MRI and 2 weeks of whatever
antibiotic you want so I
     Can go have my lunch b/c it's obvious that
WebMD has got the upper
     Hand here and I'm just too tired to debate the
issue...."
     "Actually, doc...I'm just here for my
physical......"
     "Oh..."

Hello, I'm Dr. Life, How can I help you today....?

10/25/09

ENVY

I saw you eyeing my prize
The look in your eyes.
Your name may as well have been
Bruce Banner because the manner in which
Your skin is turning green and your jaw
Muscles are flexing is all telling of
What you really mean.

I see you scooting nearer trying
To share my experience. Your hot
Breath on my arm as you pour on your charm
Like a snake coercing his prey.
Don't even look at me that way

I feel your angst as you watch me proceed.
Each move that I make increases
Your need. Now you fidget in your chair
Wanting me to invite,
Thinking the fact that I possess it
Is just quite not right.

Now I hear you whispering to yourself
You're so jealous of this gourmet wealth.
Butterflies in your stomach, salivary glands
In overdrive, I lick my lips to take that last bite,
When you try interrupt me with a little surprise.
Moving towards my sweets w lust in your eyes.

Man you better step away from my pancakes
Before you become a part of my back yard!

9/12/09

JAMILAH

My thoughts unswirl like the center of a rose
And neither their sweet scent nor does the
Soft touch of this blanket comfort me.
People die,
And though I've seen many come and go
At the hands of cellular vampires, the
Emptiness pales in comparison to
Losing one of my own.
Transition occurred but she is still with me
And I smile when the wind blows because
We run in the same soul circles; I know that
I will see her again. I dream, and I ask her to
Come visit me once in awhile; let's go to that
Place in St. Croix...that plot of land where
Your rocking chair and my hammock await.
When I need an escape, come rescue me,
Reminding me of all the times we laughed
Together, holding each others' tears and dreams
In the same hand. You remind me of why I push on.
I will embrace you the way I remember you;
Long lemongrass locs and perfect soft smile,
My sister I will remember you when I look
Into the eyes of my first born daughter;
"beautiful, lovely, graceful, elegant" Jamilah.
I cried tears of sorrow first because I miss you,
And when the tears of sorrow dried, I cried
Tears of gratitude for it was God's grace that
Allowed our souls to reunite once again for
Another brief moment in endless time.
Finally I cry selfish tears because even though I
Know that spirits come and go, I bear the gift
Of humanity and grief comes with the package.

133

But so does acceptance----and in celebration and Honor of your life, I will accept your temporary Departure from my circle and patiently await for God to allow us to meet at another crossroads... Another lifetime.

4/12/09

SIMPLE RANDOM THOUGHTS

Dr. Maiysha Clairborne

THE ANGRY DANCE

Maniacal winds howl
The branches bend to its will
Birthing an angry dance

© MTC 9/18/2005

NEON PLATEAUS

Beneath mystic haze
Hides luscious dark green forests
On neon plateaus

© MTC 9/18/2005

CINQUAIN #1

Fear

Powerful, destructive
Engulfing, paralyzing, life-threatening
The opposite of love
Trepidation

© MTC 12/2005

SENRYU #3

To Kill a Mockingbird...
Simply run the little bitches over
While they're crossin' the street

© *MTC 12/2005*

OTHER PEOPLE

Do not worry about those
who are potentially betraying you
at this moment.
They too, live in fear

© MTC 01/15/2006

HAIKU # 13

*Barren branches sway
Under the winter sunlight
Gaily together*

Mtc 1/15/07

HAIKU #14

Cold snowy winter
White powder blankets the street
What a joyful site

(co-authored by Jordan Micko)

Mtc 1/15/07

HAIKU#15

Thunder exploding
Follows a serpent white light
God shares angry tears

Mtc 1/15/07

Dr. Maiysha Clairborne

HAIKU #16

White mist separates
To reveal ancient ruins
Of a mystic world

Mtc 1/15/07

BEAUTY WITHIN

Painting their faces
Red pouting lips part
Each young face watches the other
Thinking she's uglier than most
Trying to wear a mask
Yet failing to escape what's inside

1/15/07

ROSE

Delicate, Illusive
Growing, attracting, deceiving
Makes me feel confused
Rosa Sericea

Mtc 1/15/07

ABOUT DR. MAIYSHA

Dr. Maiysha Clairborne is an internationally recognized integrative family physician, physician wellness, career, & business-entrepreneurship coach, the CEO of Stress Free Mom MD, and founder the Next Level Physicians Entrepreneur's Institute. Dr. Maiysha's more than 14 years of experience in clinical medicine & her own struggles with burnout fuels her passion not only for changing the lives of the thousands of patients over the year through her wellness programs that she has, but also to be an advocate for physicians world wide being happy and fulfilled in their careers and their lives.

Her repeated exposure to and experience with supporting burnout in physicians, as well as her own journey in conquering burnout & creating a career & life by her design is what inspired her to start Stress Free Mom MD & The Next Level Physician's Entrepreneur's Institute.

Dr. Clairborne's success with helping physicians in their lives and careers is based on 4 core principles. Through these 4 pillars she is able to empower physicians by:

1) Teaching them tools to recover from and prevent burnout

2) Helping them Discover balance in an unbalanced profession,

147

3) Showing them how they can Create a career they love on their terms, and

4) Giving them the tools to Live a Life by their design.

Dr. Clairborne also has a passion for delivering trainings, workshops, keynotes, and retreats. She has delivered her trainings in arenas such as the International Conference on Physician Health, CPR in Progress: Physician Women's Wellness Conference, and the internationally held WELLMED Physician Conference. A powerful and valuable coaching asset, Dr. Clairborne has been recruited to be a resource to such companies as The Happy MD, Vital Work Life, & Healthy Healer Program through Carolinas Medical Society.

Best known for her down to earth personality, poignant humor, and out of the box thinking style, Dr. Clairborne has turned her wisdom into two transformational books, an award-winning streaming radio show, and a wildly popular blog. Furthermore, her transformational online coaching programs and curriculums are utilized widely by physicians worldwide.

Dr. Maiysha's training journey began at Emory University completing her Bachelors in Psychology, and then went on to complete her medical degree at Morehouse School of Medicine. Finishing her Family Medicine Residency at Florida Hospital in Orlando, FL, s Dr. Clairborne has additional training in integrative medicine, acupuncture, hypnosis, neurolinguistic program, Time Line Therapy TM, and is a she certified coach and trainer. Dr. Clairborne is

Associate Clinical Professor with Morehouse School of Medicine, and a recurring guest faculty lecturer with Emory University School of Medicine. In addition to her own blog TheStressFreeMD.com, Dr. Clairborne regularly appears on award winning blogs such as KevinMD.com, MomMD, Doximity & QuantiaMD, and other online media and physician platforms.

Dr. Clairborne is currently very active in the graduate medical education community, providing her trainings on preventing burnout & creating the ideal career for students & residents from several institutions including the Atlanta Medical Center, Northside Hospital, Gwinnett Medical Center, Emory University, and Morehouse School of Medicine.

The Possibilities For Working with Dr. Maiysha

Dr. Clairborne is available for media interviews, speaking, coaching, retreats, and keynote events. Here are some other possible ways you may want to work with her:

1. Host an "Behind the White Coat: Things We Think & Do Not Say" event or discussion group for your group of doctors, residents, medical students or staff.
2. Host Your Own off site Behind the White Coat: Things We Think & Do Not Say" independent of a hospital organization or association.

3. Attend one of Dr. Maiysha's existing "Behind the White Coat: Things We Think & Do Not Say" events or programs.
4. Invite Dr. Maiysha to speak at your organizational meeting, hospital, institution, or residency retreat
5. Join one of Dr. Maiysha's Burnout to Balance Physician Wellness Courses, Programs or Events
6. Join one of Dr. Maiysha Next Level Physician's Entrepreneur & Business Courses, Programs or Events
7. Connect with Dr. Maiysha on Social Media (see social media handles below)
8. Create Your Own Customized personal coaching or organizational experience w/Dr. Maiysha

How to Reach Dr. Maiysha

1. If you are media and would like to interview Dr. Maiysha about this book or any of her endeavors or projects, please email media@drmaiysha.com
2. If you are an organization, hospital or institution that would like to have Dr. Maiysha speak at or facilitate an event, please email booking@drmaiysha.com . You may see a full list of topics & speaker list and demo reel by visiting www.DrMaiysha.com
3. If you are a physician struggling with burnout and would like to learn more about working personally with Dr. Maiysha, you may visit www.stressfreemommd.com . There

is a free webinar available on the home page, and you may also schedule a complimentary discovery call with her and/or her team.

4. If you are a physician thinking about leaving medicine, starting your own business or just want to learn how you can leverage your existing medical expertise to create a career you love by your design and on your terms, visit www.nextlevelphysicians.com and schedule a free discovery call w/ Dr. Maiysha personally.

Thank you for being the inspiration for the publishing of this book, and for reading it, spreading the word and being an active and important part of my community. I love you all!

Join me on social media!

Facebook:

Pages to Like

www.facebook.com/DrMaiysha

https://www.facebook.com/StressFreeMomMD/

https://www.facebook.com/NextLevelPhysicians/

Facebook Groups to Join:

Stress Free Mom MD: Moms in Medicine Creating a Life You Design
https://www.facebook.com/groups/stressfreemommd/

Next Level Physicians: Doctors in Business & Entrepreneurship: https://www.facebook.com/groups/nextlevelphysicians/

White Coat Movement: Doctors Are Human Too

https://www.facebook.com/groups/DoctorsAreHumanToo

Instagram

IG @TheStressFreeMomMD

Twitter

TW @DrMaiysha

LinkedIn

LinkedIn: in/nextlevelphysicians